Speed of

by Althea   pictures by Susie Pritchatt

Published by Dinosaur Publications

Fast   **faster**

fastest

Vroom, woosh, zoom.
That one was
much the fastest.

Slow

slower

They slowly plod
up the hill.

slowest

The shoppers bustle
briskly along the street.
The boy skates swiftly by.

Quick

quicker

quickest

Don't dawdle,
don't lag behind,
make haste.
We must hurry
or we will be late.

Laura wants to
loiter or linger
awhile.

Walking

jogging

running

Who will get there first?
The runner sprints
rapidly past the jogger.

Walk

trot

canter

gallop

They pretend to be
horses.

No one is
in a hurry!

potter

Trudge

shamble

amble

saunter

stroll

Plod

hobble

totter

No prizes for guessing
who will win this race!

shuffle

stagger

The children are watching
the bird hopping about
looking for food.
Ants scurry away.
The cat is creeping up
behind.

The cat pounces.
The bird flies.

Sally slithers and slides
and slinks through the sand
like a snake.

Robert spins rapidly
round and round
like a top!
He's giddy.

The tractor trundles
slowly down the road.
The traffic crawls
along behind.

It is hardly moving.
It is coming to a halt.
The sign says STOP.

Fast or slow
you get there
in the end.

Dinosaur Publications is an imprint
of the Children's Division, part of
the Collins Publishing Group

Printed by Warners of Bourne and London